Color By Number
Stress Relief

A FEW SINCERE WORDS FOR YOU

We appreciate you picking our coloring book amongst so many others. Your feedback is the highest compliment and source of motivation we could have acquired although we are aware that there are brilliant authors, who have written and released other excellent books.

BEFORE YOU GO

We hope you love our books and would genuinely appreciate it if you could share the sections you colored on social networks with the hashtags: #southernlotus #southernlotuscoloringbook #southernlotuscoloring

In addition, we are eager to read your Amazon reviews. We value all constructive comments, and we'll take them into careful consideration as we work to enhance both our books and our community.

Please feel free to reach out to us if you have any questions.
coloring@southernlotus.com

Visit our social media pages and follow us by using the code below:

This book belongs to:

....

Test color page

1
White
#ffffff

2
Light Yellow
#ffffcc

3
Yellow
#fffb68

4
Dark Yellow
#efd662

5
Light Orange
#fcdc6f

6
Orange
#f9b552

7
Dark Orange
#ea7842

8
Light Pink
#fac5e3

9
Pink
#f461b1

10
Dark Pink
#c52c63

11
Light Red
#f57c7f

12
Red
#f23c3f

13
Dark Red
#c13039

14
Yellow Green
#e9fe66

15
Apple Green
#b2cb4f

16
Moss Green
#8ba53e

17
Cyan
#49d1cf

18
Sky Blue
#c6e1fa

19
Blue
#285ddf

20
Navy Blue
#19329e

21
Light Purple
#c43cdc

22
Purple
#6831a9c

23
Dark Purple
#5d0f70

24
Light Brown
#b37c3e

25
Brown
#875c2c

26
Olive Brown
#58421d

27
Light Gray
#dfdfdf

28
Gray
#a8a8a8

29
Dark Gray
#656565

30
Black
#000000

Test color page

1 White #ffffff	**2** Light Yellow #ffffcc	**3** Yellow #fffb68	**4** Dark Yellow #efd662	**5** Light Orange #fcdc6f

6 Orange #f9b552	**7** Dark Orange #ea7842	**8** Light Pink #fac5e3	**9** Pink #f461b1	**10** Dark Pink #c52c63

11 Light Red #f57c7f	**12** Red #f23c3f	**13** Dark Red #c13039	**14** Yellow Green #e9fe66	**15** Apple Green #b2cb4f

16 Moss Green #8ba53e	**17** Cyan #49d1cf	**18** Sky Blue #c6e1fa	**19** Blue #285ddf	**20** Navy Blue #19329e

21 Light Purple #c43cdc	**22** Purple #6831a9c	**23** Dark Purple #5d0f70	**24** Light Brown #b37c3e	**25** Brown #875c2c

26 Olive Brown #58421d	**27** Light Gray #dfdfdf	**28** Gray #a8a8a8	**29** Dark Gray #656565	**30** Black #000000

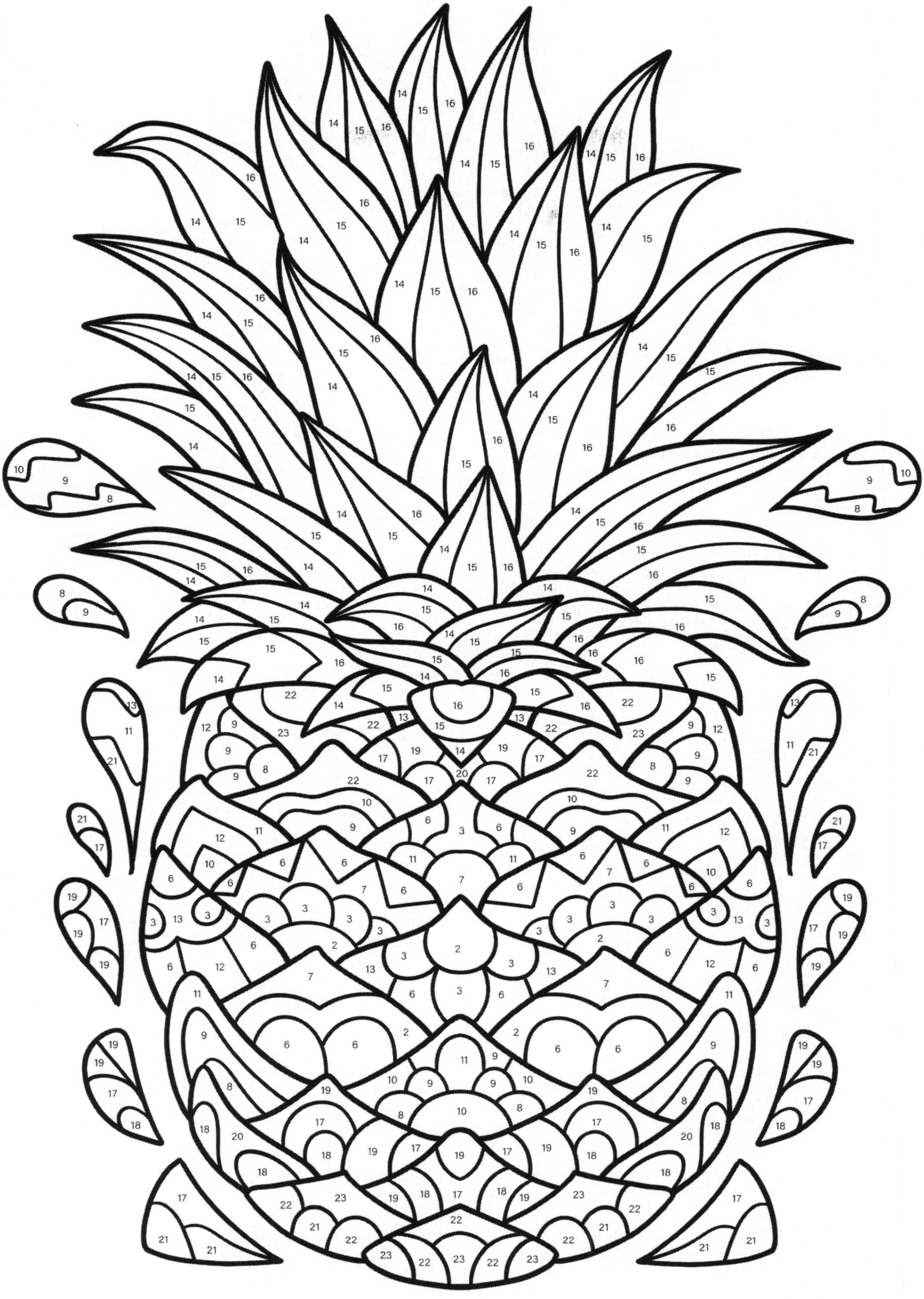

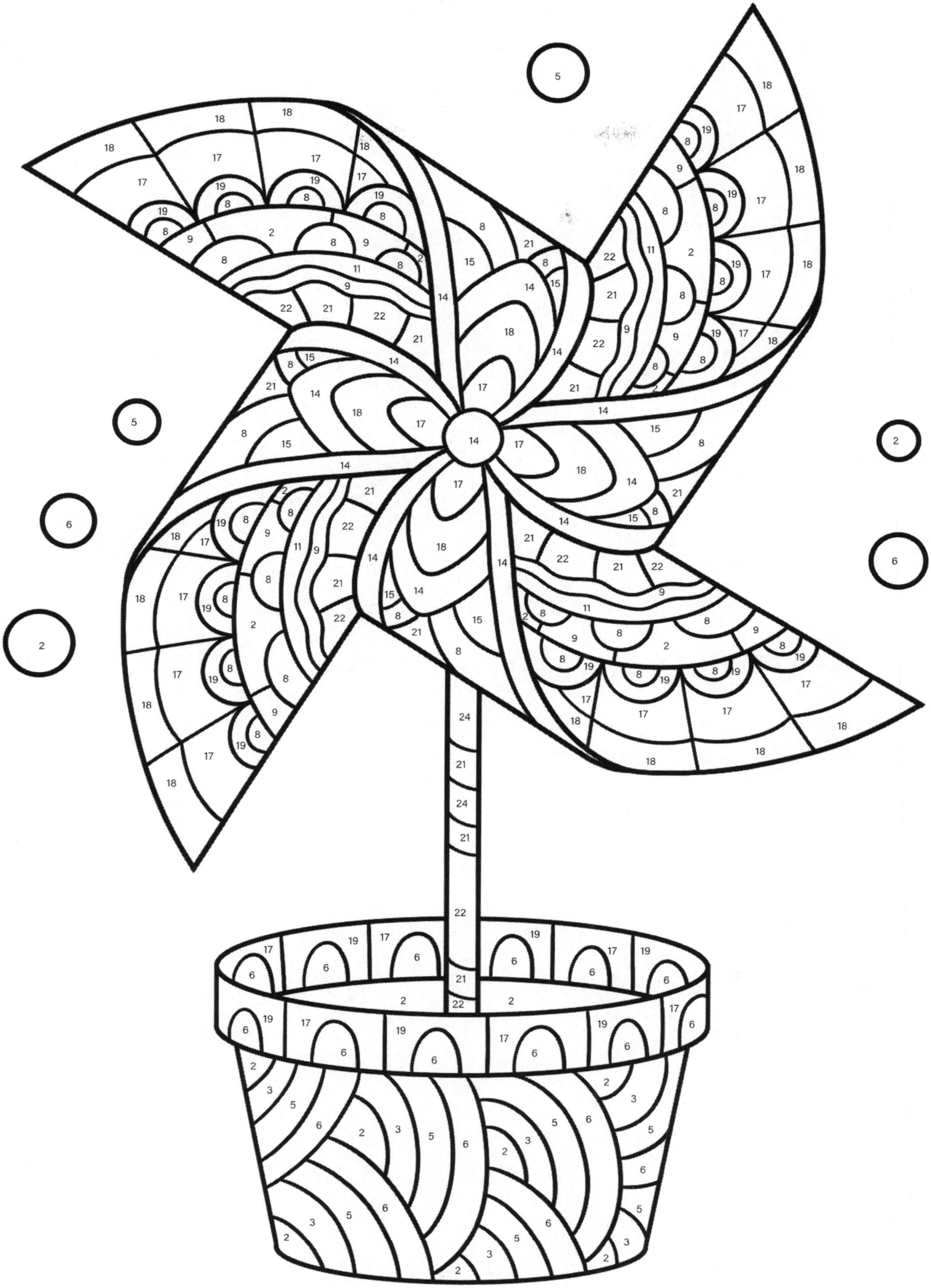

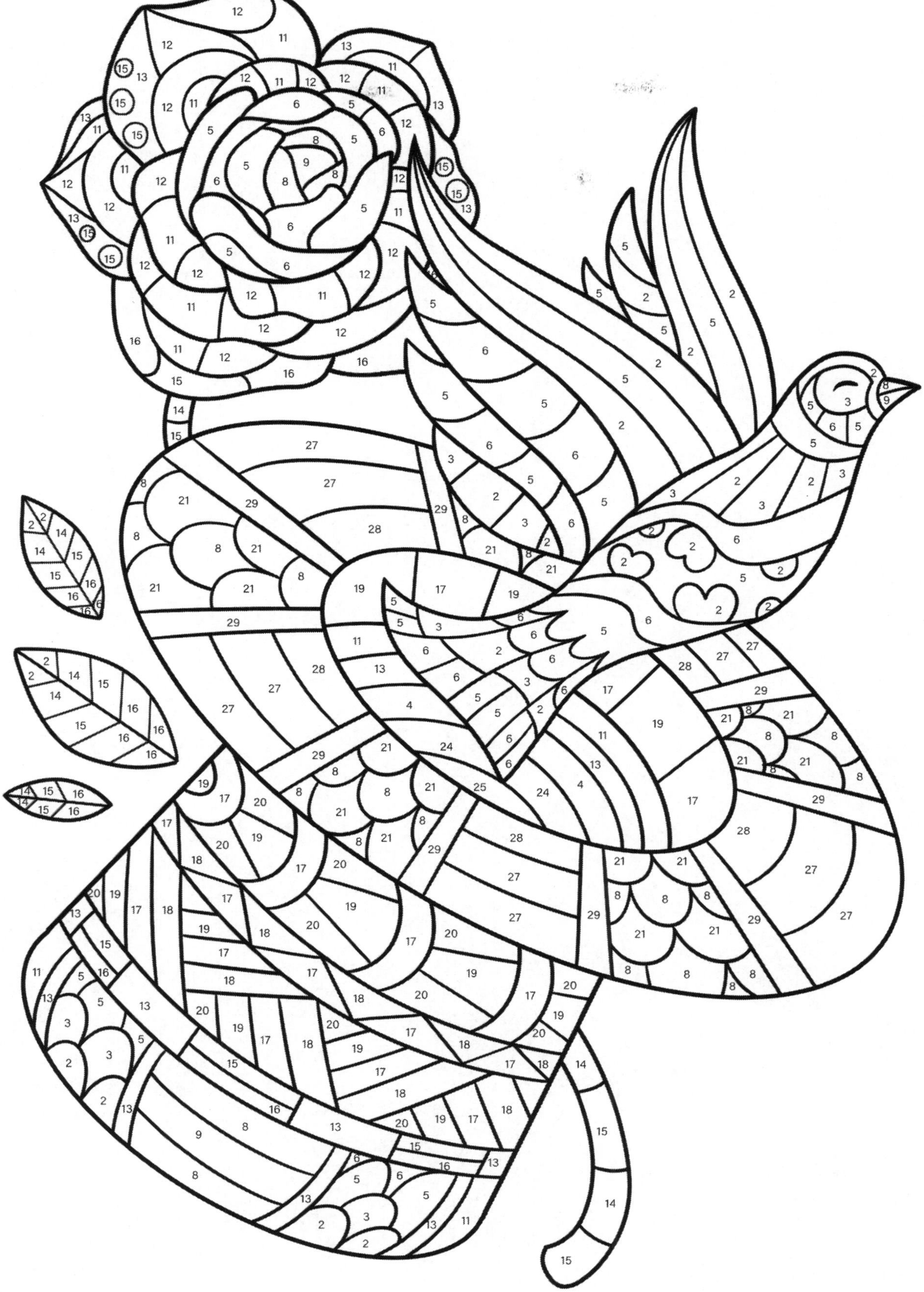

Made in the USA
Columbia, SC
21 August 2024